MW01200301

Active Shooter Response

&

Tactical Bleed Control

Training

for

Community - Families - Business

Laura J. Kendall

Important Numbers

Emergency Services - call 911 or your country specific emergency number.

Local Police Department # _____.
Local Fire Department # _____.
Local Ambulance Squad # _____.

Workplace Information

Security Department #_____.
Facility Address #_____.

In a critical situation know the following

Location Address:

Location Floor:

Location Room:

Number you are calling from #_____.

Your cell phone/ call back #_____.

What are you reporting?

Number of victims?

*Hang up when the dispatcher tells you to. Answer all their questions. You are the eyes and ears of the responding law enforcement.

Basic Emergency Treatment for a Severe Arterial Bleed

If safe to do so then call out for help!

Tell them to call 911 or your country specific emergency number or call once you are able to control the bleeding.

Apply medical gloves or something to protect yourself from blood.

↓

Perform an **RTA** to find life threatening bleeding.

↓

Arterial Bleed? - YES! - Begin self-aid or buddy-aid by applying **Direct Pressure** to the bleeding site.

↓

Bleeding does not stop with direct pressure?

Immediately apply a ↓ **Tourniquet (extremity only) or you may need to pack the wound if it is an area where you can't apply a tourniquet (neck, groin etc....) or the tourniquet is not stopping the bleeding. Continue holding direct pressure on the wound.**

Keep the victim supine & warm. Reassure victim. Unresponsive or semi-conscious victims place in the recovery position. Monitor & continue controlling the bleeding site. Do not pack the head, chest, abdomen or back!

Definitions

Immediate Responder: A person who is trained to respond, recognize and aid during an active threat.

EMS: Emergency Medical Services.

LE: Law Enforcement.

LEO: Law Enforcement Officer.

GSW: Gunshot Wound.

Cold Zone: An area where no significant danger/threat is reasonably anticipated.

Warm zone: An area close to the threat/shooting, which is not completely secure and where you have a chance of being shot.

Hot Zone: Ground zero - where the active threat/ shooting is taking place.

RTA: Rapid Trauma Assessment.

Soft Target: A person or place unprotected/unarmored and vulnerable.

Staging area: A safe area which provides cover and concealment for responders, before they enter the scene.

Tactical Trauma Care: A specific set of action steps utilized to provide immediate treatment of traumatically injured victims.

Triage: The act of sorting victims according to the seriousness of their injuries and from this treatment and transportation decisions are made.

Dedication

This book is dedicated to you, because you are taking the proactive and much needed stance of learning what to do in the case of an active threat, shooter or terror attack.

Having the knowledge and action steps to take during an incident may well save lives and change the scope of active threats forever.

Acknowledgements

I would like to acknowledge the following agencies and sites for their invaluable wealth of information on active shootings, workplace violence and treating the wounded. Please take time to go to their websites and read the information as well as watch the videos.

The Department of Homeland Security

FEMA

Ready Houston - Run Hide Fight

Texas State University - Avoid Deny Defend

The U.S. Department of Labor

OSHA

Officer Survival Solutions

Rapid Application Tourniquets

North American Rescue

TECC Guidelines

National Safety Council

LSU/NCBRT Active Threat Integrated Response Course

Foreword

I've been in the field of EMS since 1981 and a paramedic since 1986, retiring in 2018. Not in a million years did I envision the violent and hate filled world we live in today. Now more than ever, it is important to educate yourself on how to survive an active threat, shooting or terror attack and how to provide basic emergency first aid to the wounded.

Active threats aren't going away and I believe it is time to arm ourselves with the knowledge and action steps, we need in order to keep ourselves alive and safe, should we be caught in such an event. Learning to recognize, react, survive, and aid during such an event or even during a medical or traumatic emergency may well be the best gift you will ever give yourself, your employees, co-workers or family.

Laura J. Kendall, MICP (retd)

Owner: Train To Respond, LLC

www.traintorespond.com

traintorespond@gmail.com

Content

Chapter 1: Active threats, shooters, workplace violence, mass murders.

Chapter 2: Tips to survive an active threat.

Chapter 3: Gunshot/stab wounds, entrance & exit wounds, rapid trauma assessment, basic bleeding treatment.

Chapter 4: Types of bleeding, advanced bleeding treatment & active shooter kits.

Chapter 5: Sucking chest wounds, blast injuries, impaled objects, burns, hypothermia.

Chapter 6: Positioning victims.

Chapter 7: Training for an active threat or shooter.

Final Exam: Written test & practical scenarios.

Resources

Conclusion

Works sited

Appendix: Quiz answer keys.

Chapter One

The purpose of this book is to help give you the knowledge and action steps to be able to recognize that a violent event is happening, to be able to react quickly and appropriately to increase chance of survival, and then to know how to provide first aid to wounded victims.

Imagine suddenly hearing shots ring out! Would you know what to do? Would you delay acting because you are in denial an active shooting or threat attack is happening?

God forbid you are shot, stabbed or caught in a blast. Would you know how to save your own life? Lately it seems people can be enjoying a regular day when suddenly mayhem breaks loose as an active killer starts murdering people before their eyes!

Would you know the steps to take to increase your chance of survival if you suddenly found yourself in such an attack? Do you know how to aid victims bleeding from gunshot wounds, penetrating trauma or an explosion?

My hope is that this guide will help you learn what to do in the event you suddenly find yourself trapped in an active threat or are injured and have precious few moments to start self-treatments on yourself or aid another who is bleeding out before your eyes.

I strongly encourage you to attend a live, hands-on training course so you can put into practice, the action steps and knowledge in this book.

I believe that hands on training to accompany this book's information is vital and can literally mean the difference between life and death.

If you can't get to a live training course, we do offer online courses at www.traintorespond.com

We hope you'll join us!

What is an active shooter?

Homeland Security describes an Active Shooter as an individual actively engaged in killing or attempting to kill people in a confined and other populated area. In most cases, active shooters use firearms and there is no pattern or method to their selection of victims. Active shooter situations are unpredictable and evolve quickly.

The FBI definition of a mass shooting requires four or more people killed in one instance. This leaves out the multitude of other shootings where multiple people are injured or killed, but four or more people are not killed at one location

***Mass Shooting Tracer is a site from the GrC community, that tracks shootings involving both multiple individuals wounded & killed.

Active Threat

A dynamic and quickly changing event that involves one or more persons attempting to kill and wound others. This may involve the use of firearms, knives, vehicles or explosive devices.

Active Killers

Active Killers come in many forms. They include active shooters, terrorists and workplace violence offenders.

Active Shooters

An active shooter is defined as an individual actively trying to kill or attempting to kill people in a confined and populated area.

-Most use firearms.

-No pattern to victim selection.

-Pick soft targets with limited security.

-They don't go in planning to survive. Most take their own life or are killed by law enforcement.

Active Shooter/Stabber Profile

Described as:

- Usually social isolates. We have seen some team up together to commit violent acts.

- Harbor feelings of hate and anger.

- Often have had some contact with mental health professionals.

- FBI states very few have previous criminal records.

- Most have had some type of emotional hardship, bullying or loss.

Workplace Violence

Workplace violence is a complex and complicated issue and cannot be covered in-depth in this book.

It is suggested that you read OSHA's Fact Sheet on Workplace Violence and The U.S. Department of Labor's Workplace Violence Program.

According to OSHA'S 2002 Fact Sheet workplace violence is defined as:

Workplace violence is violence or the threat of violence against workers. It can occur at or outside the workplace and can range from threats and verbal abuse to physical assaults and homicide, one of the leading causes of job-related deaths. How ever it manifests itself, workplace violence is a growing concern for employers and employees nationwide.

Nothing can be an absolute guarantee that you will not become a victim of workplace violence, but knowing simple steps can decrease the possibility.

- Employees should attend a personal safety training program that will educate them how to recognize, avoid or diffuse violent situations.

- Always alert supervisors of any concerns for safety/security. Trust your gut and if you feel there is a danger take proper precautions.

Read The OSHA'S 2002 Fact Sheet workplace violence at https://www.osha.gov/OshDoc/data_General_Facts/factsheet-workplace-violence.pdf

The U.S. Department of Labor's Workplace Violence Program classifies three levels of warning signs.

View the full program at https://www.dol.gov/oasam/hrc/policies/dol-workplace-violence-program.htm

Levels of workplace violence offenders

Level One - Early warning behavioral signs a person may display.

- - Intimidating or bullying.
- - Discourteous/ disrespectful.
- -Uncooperative.
- -Verbally abusive.

Level Two - Escalation of the situation. If warranted call 911!

- - Argues with co-workers, customers, vendors and management.
- -Refuses to obey policies & procedures.
- -Sabotages equipment/steals property.
- -Verbalizes desire to hurt co-workers or management.
- - See self as a victim and that management is against them.

<u>Level Three</u> - Dangerous escalation of the situation! Call 911!!

<u>Level Three Behavior</u>

- -Intense anger.

- -Suicidal threats.

- -Physical fights.

- - Destruction of property.

- -Showing extreme rage.

- -Use of weapons to hurt or harm others.

<u>Remember</u>

- In all cases secure safety for yourself and others!

- Call 911 if it is warranted or you feel you are in danger!!

- Leave the area if you feel you are in danger.

- Cooperate with responding law enforcement.

- Notify your supervisor.

- Document behaviors you observe.

- Follow the policies and procedures set in place by the employer or corporation you work for.

It is highly suggested that you get more in-depth training and resources regarding workplace violence. This is a brief overview and does not encompass all the knowledge you need to know regarding workplace violence.

Domestic Violence

According to The U.S. Department of Labor's Workplace Violence Program there will be early warning signs of violence that is escalating outside the workplace.

A domestic violence victim may show symptoms such as:
- -Increased fear, emotional episodes, physical injury.
- -Work performance deterioration.
- By recognizing and intervening when early warning signs are evident a more serious incident may be prevented.

***If a domestic abuser shows up at work with the intent of harming the victim or others this requires a Level Three response immediately.
- Call 911 and secure safety for yourself and others

Chapter 1 ASRT Quiz

1. According to Homeland Security, an active shooter is intended on killing someone they know, i.e., a familiar.

True

False

2. The FBI definition of a Mass Shooting is: Three or more people killed in two or more places.

True

False

3. Many active shooters usually do not have criminal records and are not well known to police until after the shooting occurs.

True

False

Chapter Two

Tips to survive an Active Threat

One of the biggest keys to survival is recognizing that it is going down and you are caught in an Active Threat or Killer event.

He or she who hesitates is lost - literally!

RUN - HIDE – FIGHT

According to the U.S. Department of Homeland Security's Active Shooter - How to Respond and Ready Houston – Run Hide Fight, there are three things you can do if caught in an Active shooter situation.

1. Run!

Not running blindly, but with a plan!!

1. Know your route. Plan it ahead!

2. Leave your stuff behind. Stuff does not save lives!

3. Help others get out!

4. Stop others from heading towards the threat!

5. Keep your hands empty and arms in the air - like you are surrendering as you run out. This will help you and others exiting not get shot by responding law enforcement.

6. Follow the instructions of law enforcement.

2. Hide!

If you can't get out - Hide with a plan and purpose.

<u>Cover vs. Concealment</u>

In an Active Threat situation one of the things to think about is "what can I hide behind?" There are two types of places to consider.

<u>Cover</u> is an object or objects that are likely to stop bullets. This not only helps you from being seen, but also will protect you from bullets. Most obvious types of cover are cement walls, vehicles (engine area), steel doors etc.…

<u>Concealment</u> is basically not being seen. Concealment offers no protection. Examples of concealment are sheetrock and plywood walls, desks, vehicle doors, tinted glass, and bushes, etc.

In an Active Threat or shooter event it is important to know if you are using cover or concealment. An excellent mental exercise I do when in a building or a public place is to observe for areas of cover and concealment. When selecting cover do note that the type of firearm used will make a difference in how much protection it will provide. As we have seen in active attacks in Dallas and other places; the use of large caliber, rapid fire firearms will penetrate objects as well as cause death and devastating injuries more than smaller caliber ones.

Having knowledge of where you are moving to before you leave is important as well. Have a plan before you start to move! This is why it is important to know your surroundings. Knowing which direction windows open and what level in a building you are in is extremely essential. This knowledge is also important to let first responders know where you are and what you are reporting!

3. Fight!

<u>Fighting as a last resort!</u>

Historically Active Killers do not like confrontations. The new breed of attacker however, have the main purpose of killing and wounding as many as possible. We are not advocating purposely putting yourself in harm's way, but sometimes there is no other choice but to defend yourself. You have a right to defend yourself!

Having some self-defense skills before having to defend yourself is obvious. The time and money used to take basic martial arts training or pepper spray training can be a lifesaver. Let me reiterate that you have a right to defend yourself if you are being attacked and your life is in danger.

Don't fight fair! Your attacker isn't fighting fair and wants you dead.

You can join our free training or take an online class at www.traintorespond.com

AVOID - DENY - DEFEND

In my live and online training courses I like to use **Avoid - Deny - Defend** as a way to survive an active shooting or threat.

At the ALERRT Center in Texas State University they examined these choices (run, hide, fight) even further and found another way of reacting to an active threat situation.

They found three things you can do that have proven effective if caught in an active threat situation. What you do matters!!

You have 3 choices:

1. Avoid!

2. Deny!!

3. Defend!!!- You have a right to defend yourself!!

According to the ALERRT Center - Avoid - Deny - Defend the first step starts with your state of mind and having awareness of what is happening around you.

AVOID

1. Situational Awareness - be aware of what is going on around you.

2. Have an exit plan. (Know your exits not just the door you came into.)

3. Move away from the threat as quickly as possible.

4. The more distance and barriers between you and the threat or shooter increase survival.

DENY

When it is difficult or impossible to get away from the threat you must deny!

1. Keep distance between you and the threat/shooter.

2. Create barriers to prevent or slow down a threat /shooter from getting to you

3. Turn the lights off and silence your phone or other devices.

4. Remain out of sight and quiet by hiding behind large objects.

5. Lock the doors.

6. Be ready to react if the threat gains entry.

DEFEND

If you can't get way for the threat/shooter or deny entry, then you must be prepared to fight and defend yourself.

You have the right to survive!

I'll talk a little about mindset here. Mindset is everything in these types of attacks. You must have the mindset that "I AM GOING TO SURVIVE!"

1. Be aggressive and committed to your actions!

2. Don't fight fair!

3. You have the right to survive! You are fighting for your life!

You can learn more at <u>avoiddenydefend.org</u>

<u>My personal thoughts on how I stay alert, prepared, and</u>
<u>ready to aid the wounded during an Active Threat.</u>

<u>The number one tip I can offer is to trust your gut feeling.</u>
<u>If something doesn't feel or seem right then do not enter the</u>
<u>area or building. If already inside then take immediate action.</u>
<u>Hesitation/disbelief can literally cost you your life!</u>

Sadly, in this new day and age of violence I view the world differently than I did growing up in the 1960's, 1970's and 1980's.

Now every time I go to a public place, business, shopping venue etc... I try to take a moment to ask myself the following: If I hear gunfire or see something that my gut tells me is wrong and a threat or attack is impending what will I do?

Try these mental exercises next time you are out in a public place.

1. Ask yourself: "What is my best route of exit? Where is the closest exit?"

2. Ask yourself: "If one exit is blocked by the attacker where are the others that I can run to?"

You must run with a plan and know all the exits ahead of time. Running frantically and without a plan can get you killed.

3.Practice situational awareness by paying attention to your surroundings and the people around you.

* Is anyone acting strangely that sets off your inner alarm bell?

* Is there an odd package or back pack sitting by itself that may signal an explosive device?

4. Scope out the area. If there is no way to get out then where can you take cover?

Remember **Cover** is something that will take a bullet for you (such as a cement wall) as well as hide you from the active shooter or threat.

If you can't find cover then how will you hide to conceal yourself from view of the attacker?

Concealment will not protect you and will only offer a hiding place.

- Practice silencing your cell phone or anything that might alert the killer to your location.

Remember if there is an opportunity (the threat moves away from the area) for you to leave and exit or get to cover or safety, then take it.

If you are able to get into a room then how can you secure the door?

Does it open inward? Can it be lock? Can it be blocked with heavy objects?

If the door opens outward, can it be secure by wrapping a belt around the upper metal hinge and prevent it from opening?

Are there any windows that open and allow exit?

Remember in these events you are to shut off the lights and hide against the wall, beside the secured door so that if the attacker looks in, he/she will not see you, but you will be able to react if they gain entry.

5. Plan out that if there is a threat how will you (to the best of ability and not endangering yourself) try to alert and prevent others from entering the area or moving toward the threat or help them escape. Do not however let a person who will not move stop you from exiting.

6. Vision yourself exiting and keeping your empty hands and arms in the air! Law Enforcement don't know if you or I are good or bad! Keeping arms up in surrender will help you not get shot by the responding law enforcement officers.

7. You will call for help when it is safe to do so. If law enforcement is not on the scene, call 911 or your local/country specific emergency number as soon as it is safe.

If you call 911 inform them of the what is happening and do not hang up until they tell you to!

Remember when caught in an attack you and I are the eyes and ears of the responding law enforcement officers!!

8. Follow the instructions of law enforcement.

If you have to fight as a last resort then how will you do it?

Look around

What objects can you use to do a counter attack should it be your life or the attackers?

Do you think there any other people willing to help you?

Do not fight fair and use anything and everything can to take the attacker down. Your life depends on what you do!

Your mindset must be that you will survive!

After action reports do show that lone Active Shooters do not like confrontations. Now, I am absolutely not advocating purposely putting yourself in harm's way, but sometimes there is no other choice but to defend yourself.

Having some self-defense skills before having to defend yourself is important. The time and money used to take basic self-defense, martial arts training or pepper spray training can be a lifesaver.

Chapter 2 ASRT Quiz

1. List the three things that Texas State University say have proven effective in surviving an active shooting.

A.

B.

C.

2. Grab all your stuff before exiting during an active shooting.

True

False

3. Provide the best definition for the following:

Cover:

Concealment:

Chapter Three

Now we will start digging deep into the aftermath of an active threat or shooting. Here you will learn how you can help yourself or other victims who are injured.

Gunshot Wounds

Entrance & Exit Wounds

It is imperative that you check the victim or yourself if shot for not only an entrance wound, but an exit wound as well!

*Entrance wounds tend to be smaller.

**Exit wounds can be huge blow out wounds.

You must treat both if there is an arterial bleed.

**Sometimes the bullet stays inside the body and there is no exit wound.

During the Initial Stages of Response

Law Enforcement will enter the hot zone with the single goal of neutralizing the shooter.

Once the shooter is neutralized, they will aid victims. Until then you will be on your own and may be the first one to render aid to the victims or perform self-aid.

In the early moments of a shooting or attack literally the only ones who can save lives are the victims of the attack itself.

It is being proven each time an attack happens, that bystanders trained in active threat survival and bleed control care are saving lives! These trained bystanders are called Immediate Responders.

It is also important to note that many EMS providers are not yet part of a trained Rescue Task Force nor are they properly outfitted with ballistic gear to enter the threat to provide care!

However, if properly trained as part of a Rescue Task Force and outfitted with ballistic gear, emergency medical services will enter the warm zone (where there is a chance they could be shot) to help you, but until all EMS is trained and a part of a Rescue Task Force, they will be in a staging area until the scene is declared safe by PD.

Be alert and follow law enforcement directions.

Immediate Responders, the first question you need to ask yourself is; 'Is the scene safe?'

If the scene is not safe and you could be shot or killed, do not attempt rescue or treatment.

Your safety comes first! Always!!

Rapid Trauma Assessment - RTA

Remember to protect yourself from blood borne diseases as best as possible in these situations.

Wearing medical gloves is best!

When you come upon an injured or shot person, the first thing you will do is a rapid assessment for signs of life and for life threatening bleeding.

This assessment should take no more than 10 seconds.

Rapid Trauma Assessment

Check: Are they conscious? Can they speak?

Check: Do they have a pulse? Are they breathing?

<u>Check wrist (radial artery)</u> You will find this by pressing down with two fingers (not your thumb) in the groove on the thumb side of the wrist.

<u>If you can't feel the radial pulse then immediately check the neck (carotid artery).</u>

Hint: feel for the carotid pulse by running your pointer & middle finger down the center of the throat and about midway down slide them towards you into the groove on the side of the neck. Press down to feel for a pulse.

<u>Assess for, find, and treat and find life threating bleeding.</u>

Note: Following the current guidelines, CPR is not attempted in an area (hot zone or warm zone) that has not been declared safe and secured by police.

Bleeding Assessment

Bleeding is the number one preventable cause of death during an active shooting or threat. It is vital you find the bleeding and stop it as quickly as possible.

Steps to Perform a Bleeding Assessment during an Active Threat:

Put the victim on their back and start your sweep in this order. Keep your hands together and fingers close together (like paws) and begin to rake them down the victim's body in this order:

1. Legs front and back – can bleed to death most quickly from a femoral bleed! Heavy bleeding – apply direct pressure, a tourniquet or pack.

2. Neck (both sides) - Heavy bleeding: direct pressure, occlusive dressing, may pack if airway will not be occluded by pressure from the gauze. The occlusive – air tight seals are applied to the neck to prevent air from entering a large blood vessel and causing an air embolism.

3. Arms (both front, back and under armpit and shoulder area): Heavy bleeding – direct pressure, tourniquet, pack.

4. Torso (front and back) apply occlusive dressing over holes. **DO NOT** pack the chest, back or abdomen with gauze.

5. Head – may apply some pressure if there is no fracture or bone depressions noted. DO NOT pack the head.

This assessment is done quickly. Your goal is to locate the bleeding in 30 seconds and control it in 60 seconds!

The priorities during a Bleeding Assessment are to find life threats and treat them.

Remember the number one preventable death is due to hemorrhaging. You can save lives.

When we look at the order of the Bleeding Assessment it begins at the legs because a victim will bleed out rapidly (between 1 – 5 minutes) when the femoral artery is severed.

The Bleeding Assessment goes in order of the deadliest injuries that can be found and treated quickly and with the most impact for survival of your patient.

Basic Bleeding Interventions

Assess for and **Recognize it**. Don't let dark clothing cause you to miss this deadly injury.

Apply gloves or something to protect yourself against blood borne disease.

Apply direct pressure by holding a dressing or something clean over the wound and press down hard.

Apply tourniquet on extremities or pack the wound in areas not amendable to tourniquet application. We do not pack the head, chest, back or abdomen.

Don't get caught on the blood or injuries which can be horrific – Stop the Bleeding!

Triage

If there are multiple victims and not enough Immediate Responders, then triage must come into play.

As hard as it may be to do if there are more victims then rescuers you must move on to the one you can still try to save. One who is still alive, but may be bleeding out takes priority.

Triage is the act of sorting victims according to the severity of their injuries. The color green = uninjured (minor), The color yellow = injured but not seriously (delayed), The color red = seriously injured (immediate).

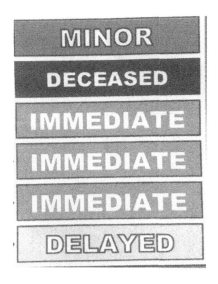

Chapter 3 ASRT Quiz

1. Start the assessment for bleeding in the arms first, as this is where a person will bleed to death, most quickly.

True

False

2. RTA stands for:

A. Run Tourniquet Artery

B. Rapid Trauma Assessment

C. Rubber Tourniquet Application

D. Rapid Tourniquet Application

3. You will easily be able to spot bleeding.

True

False

Chapter Four

Bleeding

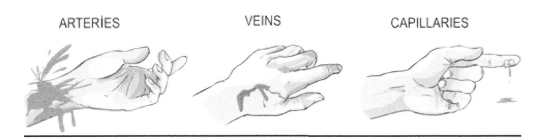

ARTERİES   VEINS   CAPILLARIES

Three types of bleeding

Capillary Bleeding

Capillaries are the smallest blood vessels and deliver oxygenated blood to the tissues and take back deoxygenated blood to the veins. Capillaries bleed slowly and it oozes out and stops quickly with direct pressure.

Venous Bleeding

Veins carry blood with little to no oxygen in them which explains the dark red color. They are not under pressure and bleed slow and steadily.

Deep cuts have the potential to cut open veins.

The best way to stop most cases of venous bleeding is to put direct pressure on the wound.

This is when a Pressure Bandage can be applied to help slow and stop the bleeding.

But remember, if it is not an arterial bleed, do not stop the pulse in the affected area. So tight with the pressure bandage, but not so tight that it acts as a tourniquet.

Arterial Bleeding – the deadly killer!

Arteries carry freshly oxygenated blood (which is why arteries have bright red blood in them) from the heart to be distributed to the tissues of the body. Because they carry rich oxygenated blood that must go throughout the body, they are under pressure. This is why arterial bleeds are so deadly.

Thankfully this is the least common type, but is the most dangerous type of bleeding.

It involves bright red blood that comes out in large volume, and in spurts that correspond with each beat of your heart.

In most cases of arterial bleeding, direct and extremely firm pressure on the wound is the best way of stopping it.

If direct pressure is not applied, a severe arterial wound can cause you to bleed to death within a few minutes.

Arterial bleeding may be hard to notice right away if the victim is wearing dark clothing or if it's a dark environment.

You will need to look at the clothing and watch for pooling of blood in one spot that seeps through the clothing.

Treat fast - you can bleed out in 1-5 minutes.

If you have attempted to control the bleeding with direct pressure and it will not stop, you must immediately apply a tourniquet to stop the bleeding in an extremity. If the tourniquet is not effective or you can't use a tourniquet (groin, arm-pit etc....) then you can pack the wound with gauze or hemostatic gauze and continue holding direct pressure.

If you do not start self-treatment or treatment of a victim with an arterial bleed from a gunshot, stab wound or other mechanism - death can occur within 1- 5 minutes!

Tourniquet Do's & Don'ts

Remember Tourniquets are for extremities ONLY

1. Place the tourniquet above the wound and never over top of a joint! (Joints in the arm are the wrist, elbow, shoulder. Joints in the leg are ankle, knee, and hip.)

2. High & Tight! Apply the tourniquet as high on the limb as possible and above the wound. Never place the tourniquet over top of the wound or on a joint!

3. Tighten the windless or tourniquet until bleeding stops and there is no distal pulse.

4. Mark the time you put on the tourniquet and tell EMS or the hospital there is a tourniquet on the victim you are with.

Current statistics are showing that applying tourniquets will not cause a person to lose their limb and have been left on for up to twelve hours without damage.

Applying a tourniquet that afterward is found to have not been necessary is acceptable, but failure to apply a tourniquet to a victim with an arterial bleed is fatal.

Types of Tourniquets

CAT - Combat Application Tourniquet

A CAT is a truly effective tool that when used correctly stops bleeding in extremities. The CAT is patented and can be applied using one hand.

Apply the CAT around and as high on the limb as possible Place it above the wound. Never place the tourniquet over top of the wound or on a joint!

The first pull on the constricting band is most important. Make the band as tight as possible around the limb.

Turn the windless until bleeding stops and there is no distal pulse. Distal pulse is the pulse farthest in the extremity – wrist, foot.

Tuck the windless in the windless clip and pull the white band over top of it.

Write the time of application on the white band.

Keep reassessing the victim and tighten or apply a second tourniquet if bleeding has not stopped.

Image courtesy of North American Rescue

To learn more, go to North American Rescue
https://www.narescue.com/

Training videos are also available on
The Train To Respond, LLC- YouTube channel.

RAT - Rapid Application Tourniquet

Rats Medical defines the RAT as: □R.A.T.S – *Rapid Application Tourniquet* – A solid vulcanized rubber core with a nylon sheath combined with a unique locking mechanism make this a simple and incredibly fast *tourniquet* to *apply* to self or others. The RATS hallmark is use under stress.

U.S. PAT. NO. 9,168,044

Image courtesy of Rats Medical

To learn more, go to Rapid Medical

https://rapidtq.com

Using a RAT

1. Hold the metal cleat.
2. Below the cleat you will see a small loop (called the three fingered loop).
3. Thread the end of the tourniquet through the three fingered loop. (Do not widen the loop to place the limb through it).
4. Now place the limb through the big loop you have created and start wrapping the band as tightly as possible around the limb.
5. The band should NOT be wrapped on top of itself, but right next to itself around the extremity.
6. When the bleeding has stopped you then put the band of the rat into the end of the cleat to secure it in place.

U.S. PAT. NO. 9,168,044

Using a Swat T tourniquet step by step

Deploy SWAT-T Tourniquet and Stretch it tight. Wrap it above the wound and as high on the limb as possible – not over a joint.

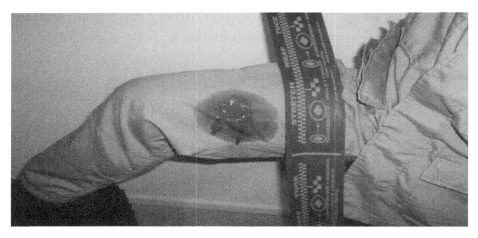

Continue the wrapping process to ensure tightness with each wrap.

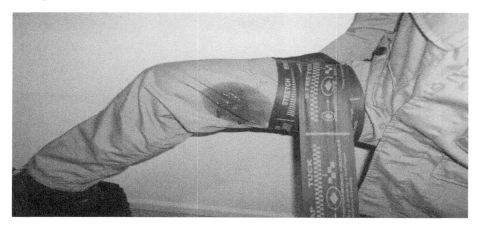

As you come to the last few inches, tuck the end of the tourniquet inside the wrap to secure it.

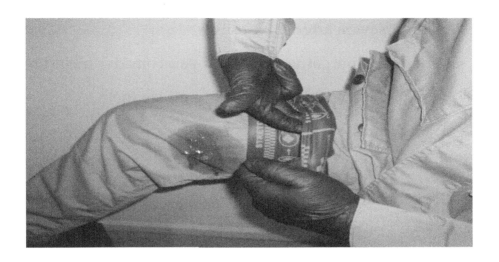

SWT: Stretch, Wrap and Tuck Tourniquet.

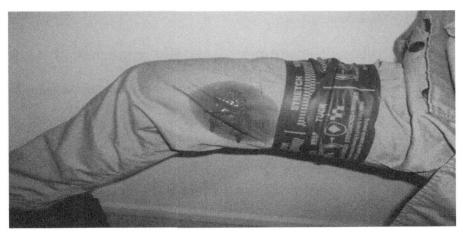

Images source: Marc Barry, OSS

Trauma / First Aid Kits

There are many different types of trauma kits specifically designed for severe arterial bleeding.

Wherever you get your kit you can consider including the following if you are trained on how to utilize them.

1. Medical Gloves

2. Tourniquet (CAT, Swat T, RAT)

3. Hemostatic Gauze

4. Pressure Bandage

5. Chest Seals

6. Disposable Emergency Blanket

Each piece of equipment is vitally important in treating a severely injured shooting victim with an arterial bleed. We will go over in depth how to utilize each piece of equipment.

A great example of a complete kit can be found at North American Rescue. They have different levels of kits – basic through advanced. Please get training on how to use all the equipment in your kit. There is no substitute for hands on practice.

North American Rescue Individual Bleed Kit

These come in both basic and advanced.

https://www.narescue.com/

Hemostatic Gauze

Hemostatic Gauze is gauze infused with a chemical agent that stops bleeding. There are several different kinds. If you are EMS, Fire or Police remember: **It must be approved for use in your state and by your agency.**

<u>Step 1</u>: Tear open Hemostatic Gauze pouch at the indicated tear notches **and take out the Hemostatic Gauze**

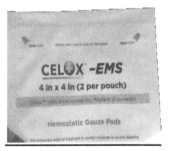

Celox and Chito Gauze is impregnated with Chitosan and works in the absence of the victim's own clotting factors by absorbing blood & fluids. This forms a gel like plug to cover the injured artery and stop bleeding.

Quick Clot – Combat Gauze is impregnated with Kaolin and helps to activate the victim's own clotting system and stop bleeding.

This may not work well in victims taking blood thinners.

Step 2: Pack the Hemostatic Gauze all the way down into the wound cavity. Making contact with the severed or torn artery

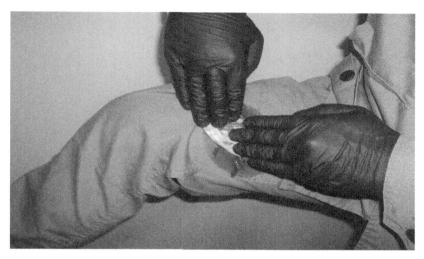

Step 3: Immediately apply direct pressure and hold that pressure for at least 5 minutes to help a clot form and stop bleeding.

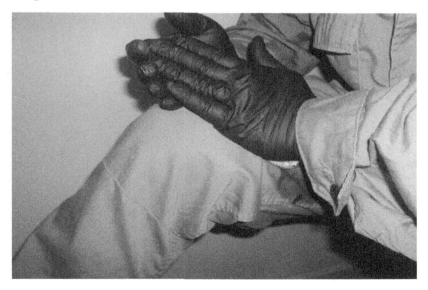

- If you use regular gauze or something else you must hold direct pressure to stop the bleeding for at least 10 minutes.

Images Source: Marc Barry, OSS

Applying a pressure bandage

__Step 1__: Apply the Emergency Pressure Bandage with non-stick pad directly over the wound.

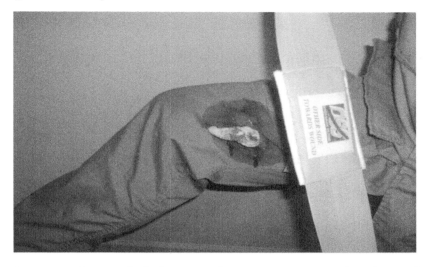

__Step 2:__ Wrap tightly creating pressure to be forced down onto the wound.

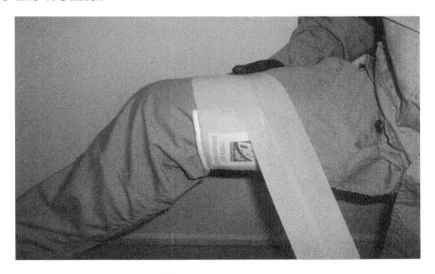

Image Source: Marc Barry, OSS

Using a Trauma / First Aid Kit

The initial assessment of an injury will help you understand what is needed and how you will treat the victim.

Keep them calm and reassure them because the faster the heart beats the more blood loss there is.

Your Rapid Trauma Bleed Assessment should take only seconds as you conduct this rapid exam, with the main goal being to find all major life threats – especially arterial bleeding!!

Remember always check for an exit wound on the victim, don't skip it, this could be deadly.

Chapter 4 ASRT Quiz

1. Bleeding is the number one cause of preventable death in an active shooter / threat attack.

True

False

2. You can bleed to death in _____ from an arterial bleed.

A. 5 - 8 minutes

B. 10 minutes

C. 1 - 5 minutes

3. You can easily spot bleeding even if the victim is wearing dark clothing.

True

False

4. Venous bleeding is a deadly killer.

True

False

5. Tourniquets are not:

A. Used only on extremities

B. Used for massive arterial bleeding control

C. Applied over a joint

6. When using Hemostatic gauze, place it lightly on the surface of the wound.

True

False

Chapter Five

Torso Wounds

Do a rapid trauma assessment of the chest, back and abdomen.

Gunshot or stab wound to the chest

Not only may vital organs be damaged, but air is now going in through the hole in the chest.

• Air from mouth/nose and the hole in chest start filling the chest cavity. This causes compression of the lungs and vital organs.

Immediate goal is to seal the chest wound.

• Remember to check for an exit wound and seal that too if found.

<u>Sucking Chest Wounds:</u> Make sucking noise as air goes in and out and frothy blood may be coming from the hole. Air follows path of least resistance.

- Victim experiences extreme shortness of breath and rapid heart rate. Lungs may collapse. Without treatment they will die.

<u>Treatment</u>

Step 1: Expose the torso.

Step 2: Look for entrance and exit wound on chest and back. Seal both.

Step 3: <u>On exhalation</u> – Cover the open chest wound with a chest seal or air tight seal (plastic wrap, plastic bag, medical glove etc...) Chest seals prevent air from going in through the hole in the chest and collapsing the lung.

*** Monitor the victim and if their breathing worsens <u>you may have to burp the seal (lift up one end as the victim exhales and then reseal) to allow air out through the valve in the chest seal.</u>

Commercial Chest Seals

Improvised Chest Seal Example

Hold or tape down all four side to make it air tight.

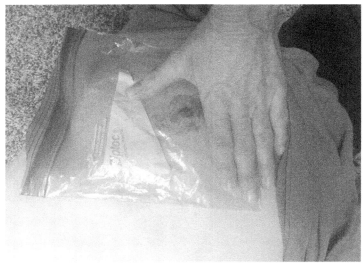

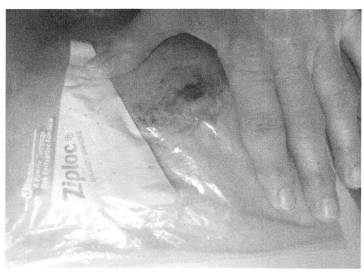

Blast Injuries

Blasts such as those from an improvised explosive device can cause massive injuries and deaths. The injuries can be very disturbing when you see them.

<u>Injuries commonly seen with blasts are:</u>

Traumatic amputations

Massive Bleeding

Impaled objects

Burns

Shock

What can you do if caught in a bombing?

If you are caught in a bomb blast the same rules apply!
Your safety comes first! Get out of the area immediately!
There may be secondary devices!
Call 911 immediately if able and tell the dispatcher your
location, what happened, injuries sustained, number of patients
and stay on the line until the dispatcher tells you to hang up.

1. Approach the blast scene with your safety in mind!

2. There may be secondary devices!!!

Scene size up

How many people are injured?
What are their injuries?
Is there a chemical component? (chemical warfare.)

Remember
It will be mass chaos – be prepared.

Begin sorting/triaging the victims according to how seriously
they are injured.

Walking wounded get them out of the scene. Let them self-
extricate if possible.

Remain vigilant against further attacks.

Traumatic amputations

Traumatic amputations – control massive bleeding!

Do an RTA – find life threatening injuries or problems.

1. Apply direct pressure.

2. Major extremity amputations may not bleed right away, but will start bleeding massively! Apply a tourniquet immediately!!

3. Treat for shock and keep them warm.

4. Recover the amputated part if possible.

Preserve the amputated part by wrapping the amputated part in sterile saline soaked gauze and place it in a watertight container or resealable plastic bag. Place the protected part in container with ice. Do not allow the amputated part to come in direct contact with ice. This will freeze the tissue and make re-attachment impossible.

In a blast injury the limb or parts may be too badly damaged to apply direct pressure on or to recover or preserve.

Impaled objects

Perform an RTA to find life threatening injuries or problems.

1. Treat life threatening problems or injuries immediately.

2. Leave impaled object in and stabilize it.

**The reason we leave impaled objects in is that the object itself may be what is sealing off the bleeding artery. To remove it would cause massive bleeding as well as further injury to organs.

3. If the object is large such as a fence it may require extrication/cutting.

4. Treat major bleeding.

Burns

Blasts/bombs can cause burns in a significant number of victims. The hot gases from the blast wave start burning the victims as soon as it makes contact with them.

Burns can be devastating to look at and may be what initially grabs your attention, but you MUST be on alert for traumatic injuries the victim has sustained and treat them as well!

Severe Burn treatment

Do an RTA to find life threatening problem or injuries.

1. Look for soot and singeing of the hairs in the nose, eyebrows, beard and look in the mouth for swelling or redness. (Do not probe into the mouth as it can cause massive swelling and cut off the victim's airway!)

2. Burns to the face = burns to the upper airway.

Manage airway by oxygenation and ventilation.

3. Stop the burn process.

You may apply moist dressings to stop the burning on isolated areas, but you do not want to cause hypothermia! Prolonged application of cold to the wound & skin can cause hypothermia which can be deadly for a burn or trauma victim.

Although we do want to stop the burning process, this is why we do not apply moist dressings or cold over large surfaces of the body. In burn victims the skin is no longer a barrier and is unable to maintain proper body temperature.

Leave blisters intact.

Once burning is stopped apply dry sterile dressing/sheets over and under patient if possible.

Transportation decisions
What type of hospital should victims go to and why?

A. Victims will be transported to a burn center unless there are traumatic injuries.

B. **Burn victims with traumatic injuries go to a trauma center first.**

Traumatic injuries always get treated first at a trauma center.

Hypothermia

It is vital to keep an injured victim warm. Even on a hot day, if they are bleeding, they are getting cold.

Our normal body temperature is around 98.6 degrees F or 37 degrees C.

When the body temperature falls below 95 degrees F or 35 degrees C a victim is considered hypothermic.

When the body temperature falls below 92 degrees F/33.3 C the body no longer can form clots to stop bleeding.

They did a study of seventy-seven trauma patients and found when their temperature fell to 89.6 F/32C there was 100% mortality.

They all died because they got cold.

Immediate Responders and First Responders can change that outcome by simply keeping the victim warm with an emergency blanket, turning up the heat, removing wet/bloody clothing and stopping bleeding.

Vehicle Attacks

Warnings have gone out from authorities that vehicle ramming attacks by terrorists are increasing in frequency.

We need only to look at the statistics and current events to see that these types of attacks are happening around the world.

Studies cite that vulnerable locations include anywhere there will be a large gathering of people.

-Sporting events

-Malls

-Entertainment venues

-Parades

-Celebratory gatherings

You must have situational awareness at all times when at a location with large gatherings of people.

In July 2016 in Nice, France a vehicle attack using a large truck killed 86 people and wounded 434 and since then there have been many more vehicle attacks around the world.

At a vehicle attack as with a large-scale active killer attack you must expect a chaotic scene with multiple fatalities and multisystem traumatic injuries.

Be alert for multi - pronged attacks! In many of the latest attacks in the US and UK the first attack is by vehicle and then the active killer leaves the vehicle and begins shooting or stabbing victims.

Situational Awareness is KEY!

If you see a vehicle crash into a crowd - approach with thoughts of a terror attack in your mind. Do not become a victim of the secondary attack.

Aiding the wounded

Please note that with vehicle attacks the scope of injuries can be wide and devastating and cannot be explained here completely. Basic bystander aid is covered.

Scene Safety

To provide basic aid to victims of a vehicle attack or any attack by an active killer you must first make sure the scene is safe.

***You do not want to become another victim.

Be alert and have situational awareness. No tunnel vision! Until the police neutralize the active killer the scene will be dynamic, unsafe and ever changing.

Immediate Responder First Aid

Can you get yourself and others to a place of relative safety?

-Perform a rapid trauma assessment to find life threats.

**If there is no pulse and you are trained to do so you may choose to start CPR.

Note: Performing CPR - current guidelines recommend this only if it is safe to do so and the active killer/s have been neutralized (Cold Zone.)

-Stop bleeding with direct pressure, packing the wound and tourniquets.

- Apply Airtight Seals to chest wounds. Look for exit wounds and seal them too.

-Keep the victim from moving, especially if you suspect a spinal cord injury.

-Keep the victim warm until help arrives. It is now being found that many victims are dying from hypothermia so keeping them as warm as possible is important.

-Comfort them. I believe that hearing is the last sense to go. I always talk to my unconscious or severely injured patients, speaking words of comfort and explaining everything I am doing.

In these horrific situations sometimes, being with them and sharing comfort and treatment to the best of our ability is all we can do for those who are badly injured or dying.

Know that you can and will make a difference to that person or animal in need.

Putting it all together

1. Recognize and react quickly to an active threat or shooter.

2. How will you get out? Plan your route of evacuation before proceeding.

3. Follow police directives. When safe evacuate the wounded to emergency medical services.

4. Identify and treat life threatening bleeding and injuries.

5. Give a full report to EMS including your treatment, tourniquet application time and location.

Remember

Active Threats, shooting and terror attacks can happen anywhere, anytime and to anybody!

Attackers are using suicide bombers or planting improvised explosive devices and causing blast injuries to victims around them.

Be on alert to the possibility. They have said they want to cause harm and death to citizens and first responders!

When in a chaotic scene have spotters to watch for potential threats as you help the wounded.

This is a new age of violence and we must be hyper vigilant!

If you see something - say something to the proper authorities.

Chapter 5 ASRT Quiz

1. The goal of treating a sucking chest wound is to seal the wound/s immediately with an airtight (occlusive) dressing.
True
False

2. Victims with a sucking chest wound experience extreme shortness of breath, rapid pulse and lung may collapse.
True
False

3. It is not necessary to check for an exit wound when someone is shot in the chest.
True
False

4.With victims of a blast if you see singeing or burns to the face be on high alert for swelling and burns to the upper airway.
True
False

5. If a victim has traumatic amputation of a limb there is minimal risk of bleeding.
True
False

6. There is usually only one blast so you don't need to be on high alert for a secondary explosion.

True

False

Chapter Six

Positioning Victims

Because every situation is different and I can't be there with you I want to let you know about accepted patient positions to consider when deciding how to best position the victim during treatment.

National Safety Council First Aid training recommends the following:

Recovery Position

In an Active Threat place an unconscious, but breathing victim into the recovery position.

Recovery position is one in which you extend the victims arm above their head and then carefully roll the victim onto their side (same side as the extended arm) allowing the victim's head to be supported by the extended arm.

Bend both legs to help stabilize the victim in this position.

Open the victim's mouth to allow drainage of blood and fluids.

The Recovery Position

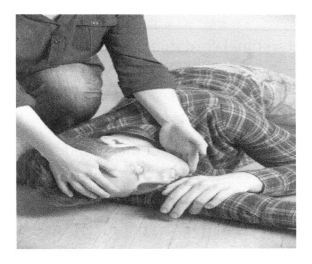

Keep reassessing and reassuring the victim. I believe an unconscious person can still hear what we say to them.

Shock Position

Responsive/conscious victims in shock from bleeding: can be positioned on their back to help stabilize them. Control bleeding and keep them warm.

Unresponsive victims with no evidence of spinal trauma and bleeding controlled should be placed in the recovery position. Keep them warm. Continue to reassess.

Spinal Motion Restriction

If you suspect a spinal cord injury then you can initiate the Spinal Motion Restriction position.

Responsive victim:
1. Explain that they need to hold their head still to prevent spinal movement.
2. Hold the victims head and neck with both hands in the position they are found to prevent movement of the neck and spine.

Unresponsive victim: Hold the victims head and neck with both hands in the position they are found to prevent movement of the neck and spine.
Open the airway with the Jaw Thrust Maneuver.
Continue to hold stabilization until help arrives

Chapter Seven

Preparing for the arrival of First Responders

It is good to know the information the emergency responders will need to know upon their arrival.

Try to have the following pertinent information written down, to give to the emergency responders when they arrive.

1. Patient's full name.

2. Patient's age and date of birth.

3. Do not resuscitate order – legal document containing the patient's wishes in life threatening situations.

4. Patient's medical history.

5. Patient's medications. - have these written down clearly.

   **Do not hand the first responders a bag or box full of various medication bottles they have to search through as this can slow down care and departure from the scene.

6. Patient's allergies

7. What happened? Paint the arriving first responders a clear picture of what is wrong or what happened to the victim or yourself.

The emergency providers will start asking questions.

Be prepared to answer the same questions and other ones as higher-level providers arrive and take over patient care.

The questions asked are in the quest to get a complete and detailed picture of the patient's condition.

A clear picture of what is wrong will assist the emergency responders in their treatment and decision making for the patient.

A good way to remember the basic information emergency responders need is the acronym is the word – SAMPLE

SAMPLE

S – Signs and Symptoms the patient is having or has had before help arrived.

A - Allergies the patient has.

M - Medications the patient is taking.

P - Pertinent medical history of the patient.

L - Last oral intake. This is very important if the patient is facing immediate surgery for their condition.

E - Events leading up to the current illness or injury. What happened before the emergency responders arrived?

Know Your Emergency System

In New Jersey where I practiced there is a tiered emergency response.

First Responders: Police officers, Firefighters, or First Aid personnel who provide oxygen and basic care until other responders arrive. Their initial interventions can mean life or death for the patient until more advanced emergency responders arrive.

Emergency Medical Technicians: A provider trained in basic life support. EMT's duties include – patient assessment, determining if advanced life support is needed, administering oxygen and some medications, spinal immobilization, extrication, bandaging and splinting, bleeding control, and emergency vehicle operations. Many EMTs are unselfish volunteers who provide emergency care to their communities free of charge.

Paramedics: A provider trained in advanced life support. Paramedics are able to assess patients and determine their condition. They then provide advanced interventions.

Advanced interventions include - intravenous fluids, endotracheal intubation, medication administration, rapid sequence intubation using sedation and paralytics, chest needle decompression, intraosseous infusions, nebulizer treatments, emergency tracheotomies, 12 lead EKG interpretation, and emergency vehicle operations. Their quick thinking and critical decisions can mean the difference between the patient living or dying.

EMTs and Paramedics may drive ambulances, but gone are the days of being called an 'ambulance driver'.

It is important to know the certification level of the emergency providers in your area. Emergency training and level of care are not the same in each state. Know who is coming to help you!

Dispatch Centers

In New Jersey we have a comprehensive 911 dispatch system.

Most dispatchers are highly trained first responders and are your life link when an emergency occurs. They are often overlooked in the chain of emergency care, but I for one believe they are the most important. Without that link to a trained dispatcher no help is coming!

Many dispatchers are trained to provide direction in medical/traumatic emergencies and can help talk you through providing the initial care.

It is important you stay calm, listen to the dispatcher, answer all questions and do not hang up until they tell you to!

Chapter Eight

Training for an Active Threat

If vs. WHEN

You must approach your preparation and training for active threat, not from a passive; "If position," but from the position of "WHEN."

It has been said that: "You do not rise to the occasion in combat, you sink to the level of training."

It is quickly becoming the standard to provide Active Threat and Bleed Control Training for companies, organizations, groups, entertainment venues, schools and places of worship.

Any place that is a soft target or has large groups of people needs to prepare and train for Active Threat events.

Have the people in your company, group, place of worship, entertainment venue, gun range, club or organization been properly trained on how to react to survive and help the wounded should an active threat or shooter attack occur?

Our training will give you and your people the skills and empowerment to step up and save lives.

At Train To Respond, LLC we offer customized in-person training workshops with lectures and hands on practice for Active Threat Response and Tactical Trauma Care.

We also offer online training courses at www.traintorespond.com

Our training is available for businesses, corporations, families, communities, groups, organizations, entertainment venues, places of worship, gun ranges & clubs and schools.

Contact us today at traintorespond@gmail.com

To learn more or take one of our online training classes please visit https://www.traintorespond.com

In- Person Active Shooter Response & Bleed Control Training

We come to your location/s and are happy to travel across the United States to bring this empowering knowledge and skill set to your people!

Until we meet again or for the first time, please remember to be aware of your surroundings at all times, know your exits always and if you see something - say something!

Be safe.

Peace,

Laura J. Kendall, MICP (Retd)

ASRT Final Exam

Grab a pencil or pen and test your knowledge.

1. List the three types of bleeding.

1.

2.

3.

2. _____ bleeding can kill you within

1 - 5 minutes if not treated.

3. List two ways to control bleeding.

1.

2.

Multiple Choice - Circle your choice

4. Venous bleeding is not:

A. Slow and steady flow

B. Dark red in color

C. Spurting out with each beat of the heart

5. When you apply a tourniquet you should tell EMS the following:

A. Time you place tourniquet on

B. Location of tourniquet

C. Why you applied a tourniquet

D. All of the above

6. What critical items can be included in an active shooter kit:

A. Tourniquet

B. Pressure Bandage

C. Hemostatic gauze or agent

D. PPE - gloves

E. Chest Seals

F. Rescue Blanket

G. All of the above

True or False

7. All EMS are part of a rescue task force and trained to enter the warm zone to provide care at an active shooting or threat?

T_____

F_____

8. You can easily spot an arterial bleed even through dark clothing.

T_____

F_____

9. You should keep your active shooter kit or a tourniquet with you at all times.

T_____

F_____

10. A sucking chest wound does not need to be sealed to prevent air going into the chest.

T_____

F_____

Answer Key

1. Venous, arterial, capillary.

2. Arterial bleeding.

3. Direct pressure, Tourniquet, Packing.

4. C -Spurts out with each beat of the heart.

5. D - all of the above.

6. G - all of the above.

7. F.

8. F.

9. T.

10. F.

Practical Scenarios

Scenario 1

You are in a meeting and suddenly you hear screaming and a crowd of co-workers are running towards you. Shots ring out behind them and you watch as several fall to the ground.

Scenario 2

You are attending an office party when two co-workers start fighting. One pulls out a knife and stabs the other in the chest. The perpetrator flees the scene leaving the knife sticking out of the second man's chest. He stumbles and collapses to the ground

Scenario 3

You are out with your family eating at a local restaurant. Outside you hear gunshots ring out and people screaming. What is your action plan to help yourself and family survive?

Resources

FEMA Is - 907 - Active Shooter: What you can do.

https://emilms.fema.gov/IS907/ASo1.

<u>You Tube</u>

Arterial Bleeding - leg: the dexitvideo.

Ready Houston - Run - Hide - Fight - Surviving an active
  shooter event.

ADD - avoiddenydefend.org

Conclusion

Thank you for investing in yourself, your family, friends, co-workers, business or organization. Together we can change the future of our world.

Together we can make a difference and empower ourselves and others when confronted with acts of violence or active threats.

Please be safe out there and as I always say; "I'm happy you have this information, but I pray you never need to put it into action!"

Peace & out,

Laura

P.S. You can always reach out to me for further information or to schedule an Active Threat Response & Tactical Trauma Care for your community, family or company.

I can be reached most easily by email - traintorespond@gmail.com.

Works cited

1. Homeland Security - Office of Health Affairs - June 2015 First Responder Guide for Improving Survivability in Improvised Explosive Device and/or Active Shooter Incidents.

2. Homeland Security - Active Shooter Preparedness.

www.dhs.gov/active-shooter-preparedness

3. Mass Shooting Tracker - This site counts the number of people shot rather than only the number killed and is updated as shootings happen.

www.shootingtracker.com

4. Global Research - Mass Shootings in America: A Historical Review.

5. ALERRT Center Texas State University - ADD

6. Pictures courtesy of Officer Survival Solutions., North American Rescue & Rats Medical

7. The U.S. Department of Labor's Workplace Violence Program.

8. OSHA's Fact Sheet on Workplace Violence.

Appendix

Quiz Answer Keys

Chapter 1 Quiz

1. False.

2. False.

3. True.

Chapter 2 Quiz

1. Avoid - Deny - Defend.

2. F

3. Cover: Hiding behind an object that will conceal you and is strong enough to take a bullet for you.

Concealment: Quietly hiding from the shooter. Shooter may spot you. Keep silent. Silence phone.

Chapter 3 Quiz

1. False.

2. B.

3. False.

Chapter 4 Quiz

1. True.

2. C.

3. False.

4. False.

5. C.

6. False.

Chapter 5 Quiz

1. True.

2. True.

3. False.

4. True

5. False

6. False

Made in the USA
Middletown, DE
18 September 2024

60532542R00064